FANTASTIC FASHION
ORIGAMI

Party Clothes

PowerKids
Press

CATHERINE ARD

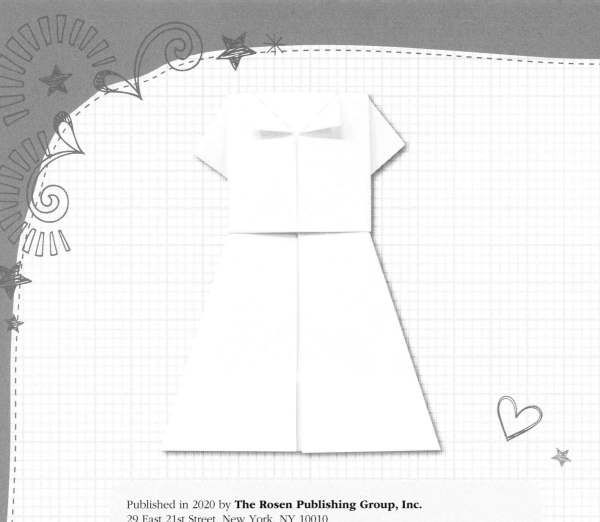

Published in 2020 by **The Rosen Publishing Group, Inc.**
29 East 21st Street, New York, NY 10010

Cataloging-in-Publication Data

Names: Ard, Catherine.
Title: Party clothes / Catherine Ard.
Description: New York : PowerKids Press, 2020. | Series: Fantastic fashion
origami | Includes glossary and index.
Identifiers: ISBN 9781725302907 (pbk.) | ISBN 9781725302921 (library bound)
| ISBN 9781725302914 (6 pack)
Subjects: LCSH: Origami--Juvenile literature. | Paper work--Juvenile literature.
| Fashion--Juvenile literature. | Clothing and dress--Juvenile literature.
Classification: LCC TT872.5 A73 2019 | DDC 736.982--dc23

Models and photography by Michael Wiles
Written by Catherine Ard
Designed by Picnic
Edited by Kate Overy and Joe Fullman

Manufactured in the United States of America

CPSIA Compliance Information: Batch CSPK19: For Further Information contact Rosen Publishing,
New York, New York at 1-800-237-9932.

Contents

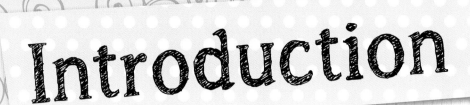

Introduction

This book shows you how to create a gorgeous collection of mini fashions. All you need for each item is a square of paper, your fingers, and some clever creasing. So, forget sewing and get folding!

Getting started

The paper used in origami is thin, but strong, so that it can be folded many times. You can use ordinary scrap paper, but make sure it's not too thick.

A lot of the clothes in this book are made with the same folds. The ones that appear most are explained on these pages. It's a good idea to master these folds before you start.

Key

When making the clothes, follow this key to find out what the lines, arrows, and symbols mean.

mountain fold ....

valley fold – – – – – – – – – – –

step fold (mountain fold and valley fold next to each other)

direction to move paper

direction to push or pull paper ▶

hold paper in place ☞ with finger

Mountain fold

To make a mountain fold, fold the paper so that the crease is pointing up at you, like a mountain.

Valley fold

To make a valley fold, fold the paper the other way, so that the crease is pointing away from you, like a valley.

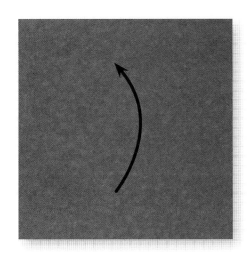

Step fold

The step fold creates a zigzag, or step, in the paper. It is used to divide different parts of a garment, such as the skirt and bodice of a dress.

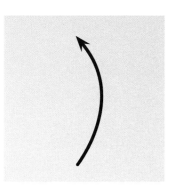

1 First fold a piece of paper in half, from bottom to top, to make a valley fold.

2 Now unfold.

3 Next make a mountain fold above the valley fold you have just made.

4 Push the mountain fold over the valley fold and press it flat. You now have a step fold.

A step fold like the one here, with the mountain fold above the valley fold, is shown like this.

A step fold with the mountain fold below the valley fold is shown like this.

Pleat fold

Once you have mastered a step fold, making a pleat is easy. In this book, step folds are always horizontal and pleats are vertical. A pleat fold uses some creases that have been made in earlier steps.

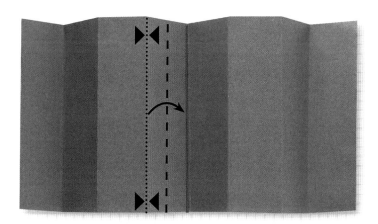

1 To make the first side of a pleat, pinch the crease shown between your fingers. Fold it over to the right until it lines up with the crease indicated. Press it flat to make a valley fold in the paper underneath.

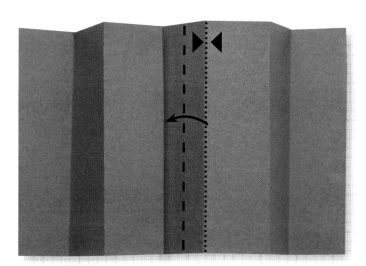

2 Repeat on the other side. Pinch the crease shown and fold it over to the left until it lines up with the crease indicated. Press it flat to make a valley fold underneath.

Hold the paper up and the finished pleat will look like this from the side.

Blouse

Step out in style with this cute, short-sleeved blouse. Choose a pretty pink or pastel paper and follow the steps to fold a dainty collar and cuffs.

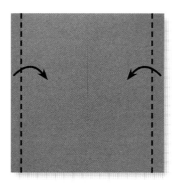

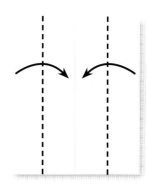

1 Fold the paper in half from left to right.

2 Fold in a ½-inch (13 mm) section on both sides.

3 Turn the paper over.

4 Fold the edges in to meet the central crease.

5 Make two angled creases as shown. When folded over the edges should be straight.

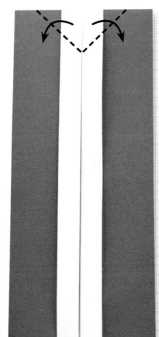

6 Shape the shoulders with mountain folds. Now make angled creases from the bottom corners.

7 Turn the paper over.

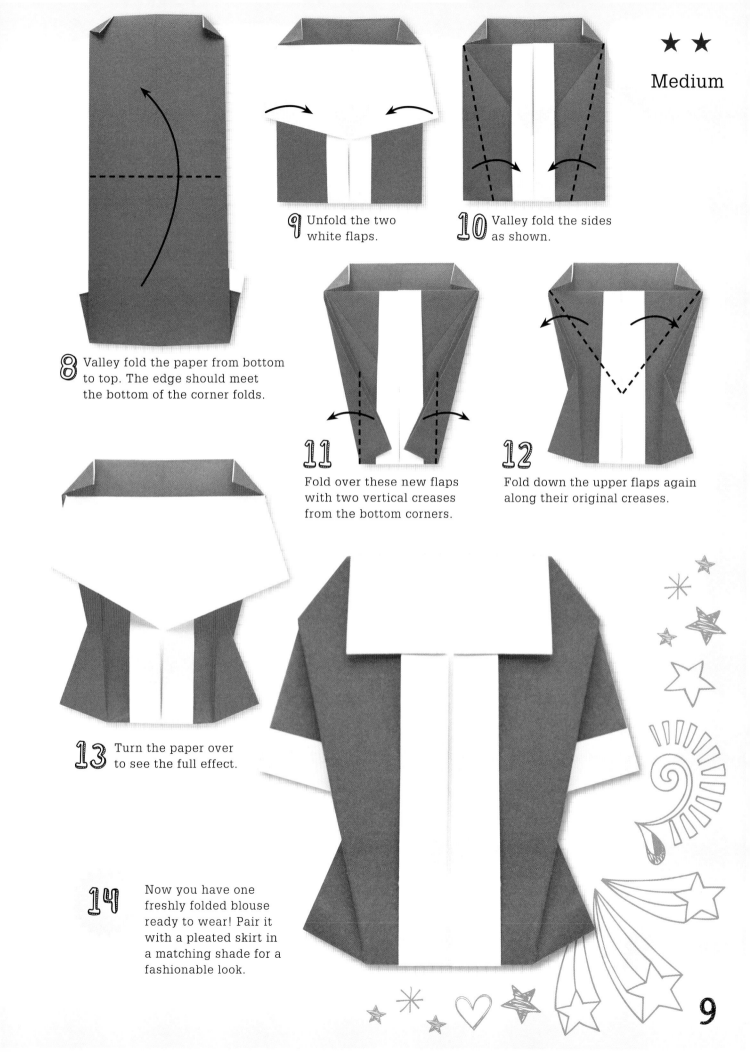

9 Unfold the two white flaps.

10 Valley fold the sides as shown.

8 Valley fold the paper from bottom to top. The edge should meet the bottom of the corner folds.

11 Fold over these new flaps with two vertical creases from the bottom corners.

12 Fold down the upper flaps again along their original creases.

13 Turn the paper over to see the full effect.

14 Now you have one freshly folded blouse ready to wear! Pair it with a pleated skirt in a matching shade for a fashionable look.

Summer Dress

It takes just a few minutes of folding to create this fabulous, bright summer dress. Use different papers to create a whole summer wardrobe.

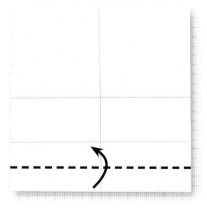

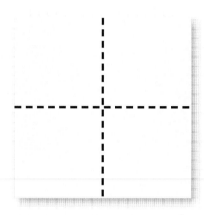

1 Fold the paper left to right and unfold. Then fold it top to bottom and unfold.

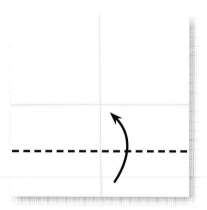

2 Make a valley fold on the bottom half of the paper.

3 Fold the bottom edge of the paper up to the central crease, then unfold.

4 Make another crease halfway between the bottom of the paper and the valley fold.

10

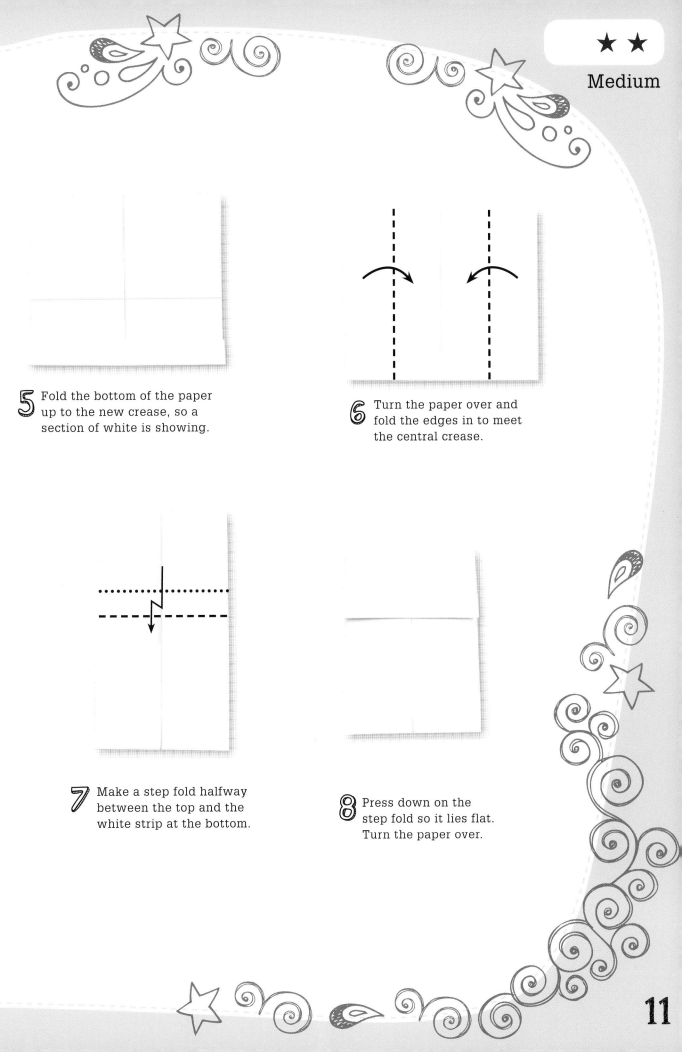

5 Fold the bottom of the paper up to the new crease, so a section of white is showing.

6 Turn the paper over and fold the edges in to meet the central crease.

7 Make a step fold halfway between the top and the white strip at the bottom.

8 Press down on the step fold so it lies flat. Turn the paper over.

9 Make two angled creases in the middle edge, as shown.

10 Fold along the creases to make two triangular shapes.

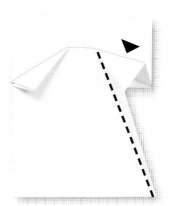

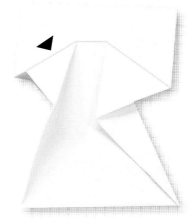

11 Make a new fold from the triangle tip to the bottom corner. Press down on the crease, as shown.

12 Repeat on the other side, folding from the tip of the triangle to the bottom corner. Press down on the top crease as shown.

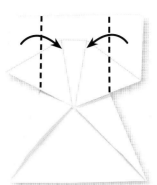

13

Fold in the edges so they meet at the central crease.

14

Make two new creases in the top section as shown.

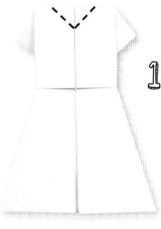

16

To make the neck, make two new angled creases that meet in a V in the middle.

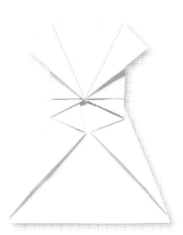

15

Turn the paper over. Your dress is nearly complete.

17

Fold along the creases, making sure the bottom edges are straight. Your new dress is now ready for that important summer party!

Party Dress

Finding the perfect dress for a party couldn't be easier! With its tiny waist and full, swishing skirt, this one is sure to be a hit on the dance floor.

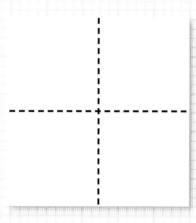

1 Fold the paper from top to bottom and unfold. Then fold from left to right and unfold.

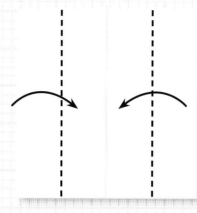

2 Fold in the edges to meet the central crease.

3 Open out the paper and turn it over.

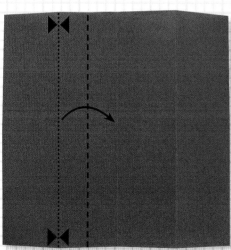

4 Now make a pleat. Take the crease on the left to meet the central crease.

5 Press flat to crease the paper underneath.

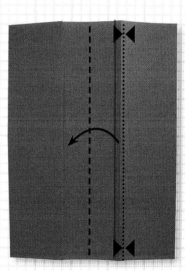

6 Repeat on the other side, taking the crease on the right to meet the central crease. Press flat.

7 You should now have a pleat down the middle of the paper, like this. Turn the paper over.

8 Step fold the paper from top to bottom around ¼ inch (6 mm) above the central crease.

9 Press down on the step fold so that it lies flat. Turn the paper over.

10 Put your finger where the edges meet and pull the pleat to the side to reveal the paper underneath.

11 Press down on the top crease as shown to make a new angled crease. Repeat on the other side.

12 Make two angled creases at the top that meet in a V in the middle. Make sure the bottom edges are straight.

13 Unfold these new creases.

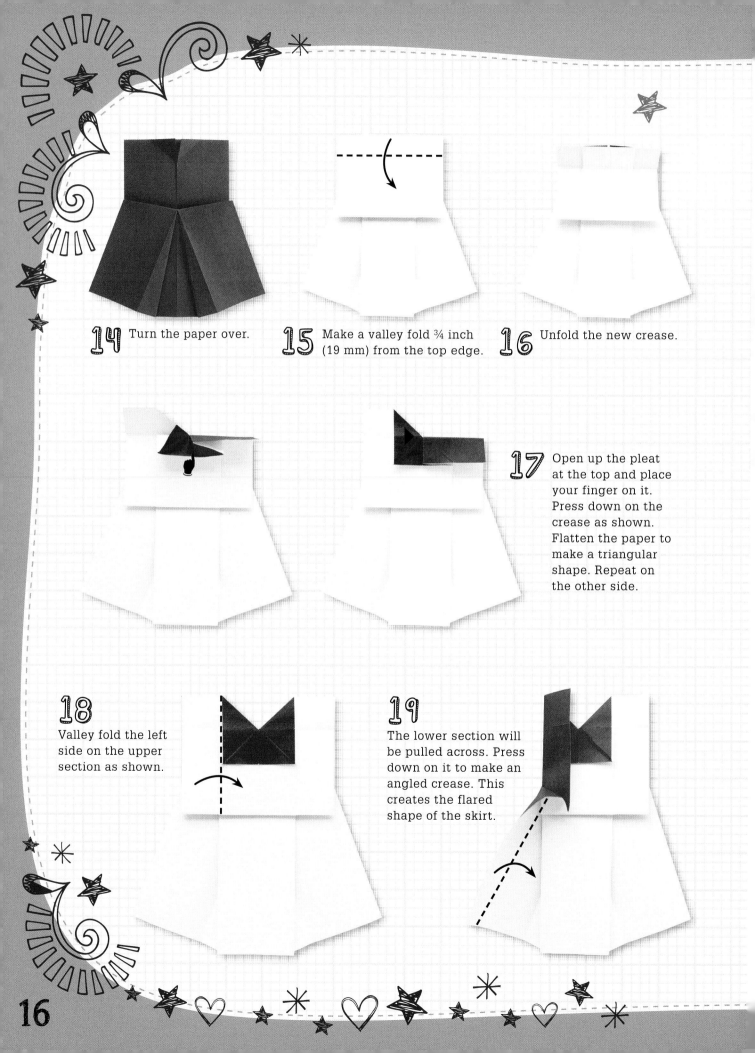

14 Turn the paper over.

15 Make a valley fold ¾ inch (19 mm) from the top edge.

16 Unfold the new crease.

17 Open up the pleat at the top and place your finger on it. Press down on the crease as shown. Flatten the paper to make a triangular shape. Repeat on the other side.

18 Valley fold the left side on the upper section as shown.

19 The lower section will be pulled across. Press down on it to make an angled crease. This creates the flared shape of the skirt.

20
Repeat on the other side, folding in the upper section and making an angled crease on the lower section.

21 Valley fold the upper sections from the outer to the inner corners to make the sleeves.

22
Turn the paper over to see the finished dress.

23
This frock is ready to rock! It's perfect for twirling the night away.

Party Coat

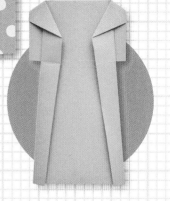

Fold this classy coat to wear over a party dress or a long evening gown. It's the perfect way to keep out the cold on chilly nights on the town.

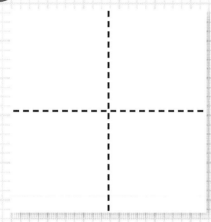

1 Fold the paper from top to bottom and unfold. Then fold from left to right and unfold.

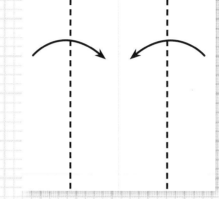

2 Fold in the edges to meet the central crease.

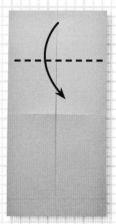

3 Now fold down the top edge to meet the central crease.

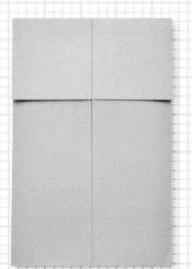

4 Turn the paper over.

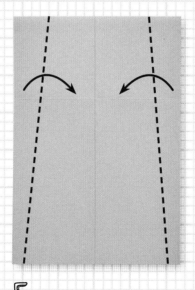

5 Make an angled crease on either side and fold in the edges.

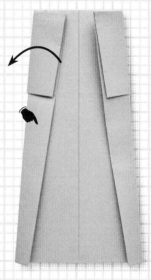

6 Hold down the lower part of the left-hand flap with your finger and open up the top corner.

7 Press down on the crease on the top edge and flatten the paper to make a triangular shape. This is a sleeve and collar!

8 Repeat on the other side. Try to make the points of the collar match.

9 Mountain fold a narrow strip along the edges of the sleeves.

10 Your stylish new coat is ready. Don't forget your party invitation on your way out the door!

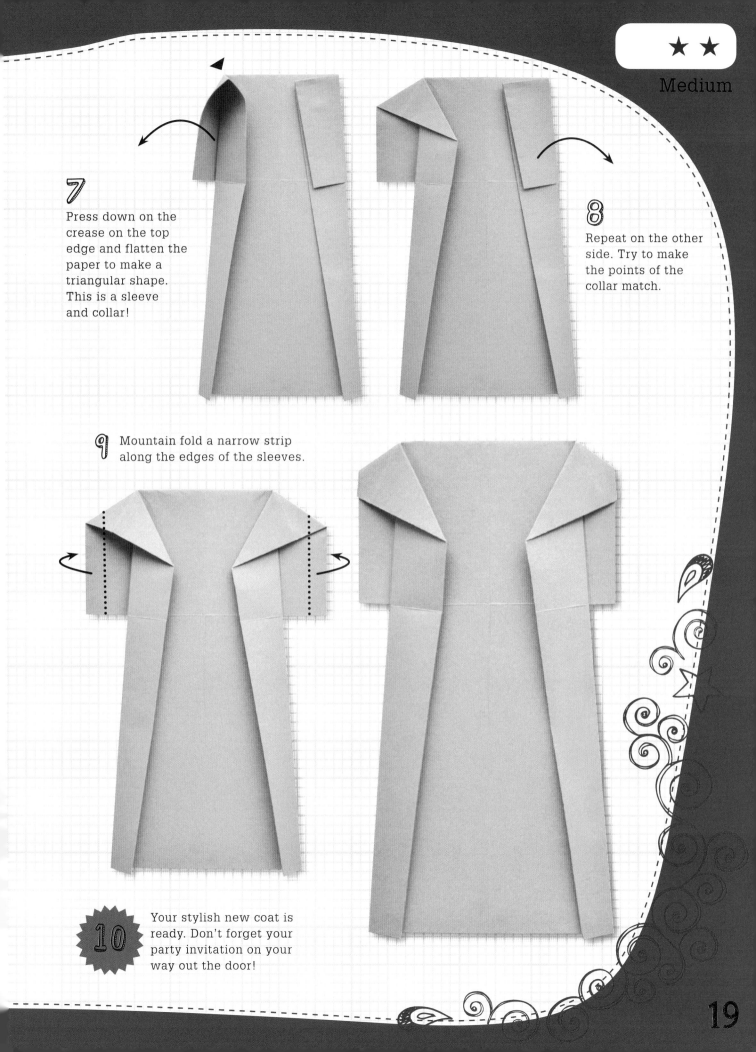

Evening Gown

This dazzling evening gown is made for glittering balls and glamorous parties. Choose midnight blue or deep purple for a totally elegant look.

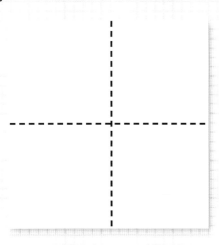

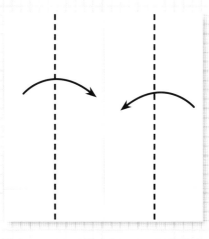

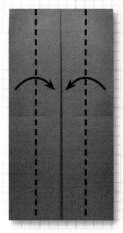

1 Fold the paper from top to bottom and unfold. Then fold from left to right and unfold.

2 Fold the edges in to meet the central crease.

3 Fold the edges in again to meet the central crease.

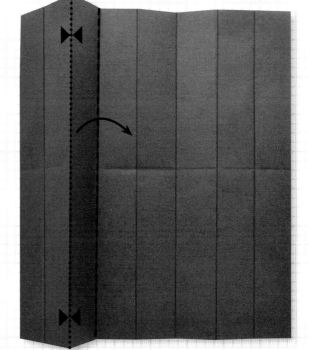

4 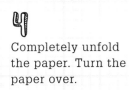 Completely unfold the paper. Turn the paper over.

5 Now make a pleat. Take the second crease from the left to meet the central crease. Fold flat.

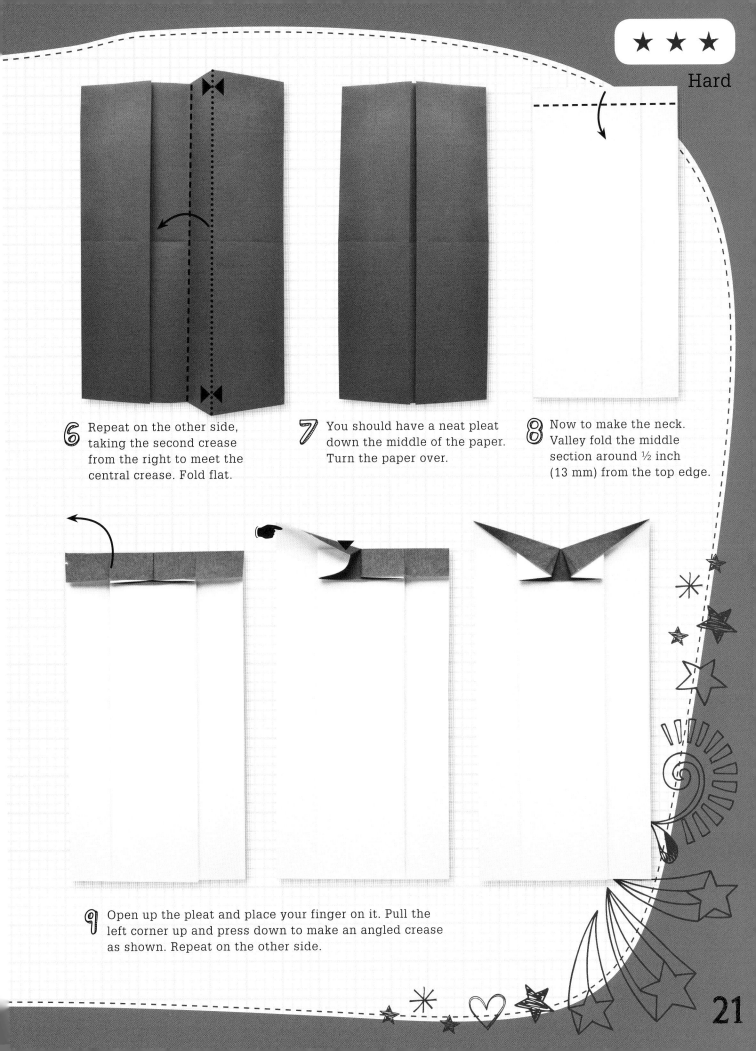

6 Repeat on the other side, taking the second crease from the right to meet the central crease. Fold flat.

7 You should have a neat pleat down the middle of the paper. Turn the paper over.

8 Now to make the neck. Valley fold the middle section around ½ inch (13 mm) from the top edge.

9 Open up the pleat and place your finger on it. Pull the left corner up and press down to make an angled crease as shown. Repeat on the other side.

10 Fold in the left and right edges to meet the central crease.

11 Make angled creases from the middle to the bottom corners. This is the skirt.

12 Create the waist with a step fold across the middle of the paper.

13 Press down on the step fold so that it lies flat.

14 Now shape the waist. First make an angled crease on the upper section, as shown.

15 Repeat step 14 on the other side.

16 Pinch the corner between your fingers and fold it over. Press down firmly on the edge of the lower section to make a new crease.

17 Repeat step 16 on the other side.

18 Turn the paper over to see the finished dress.

19 This gorgeous evening gown is ready to sweep down the red carpet.

Smart Suit

Make your creases extra sharp and your folds totally flawless for this snappy two-piece suit.

PART 1

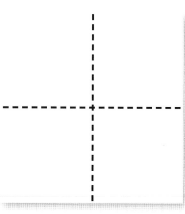

1. Fold the paper in half from top to bottom and unfold. Then fold from left to right and unfold.

2. Mountain fold a narrow strip on the top edge. This will be the sleeve cuffs.

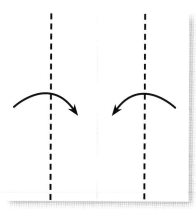

3. Fold the edges in to meet the central crease.

4. Make two angled creases that meet in a V, as shown. When folded back, the tips of the flaps should meet the edges of the paper.

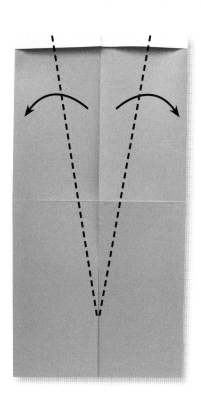

5. Turn the paper over.

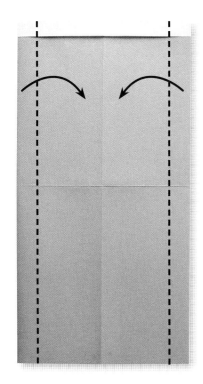

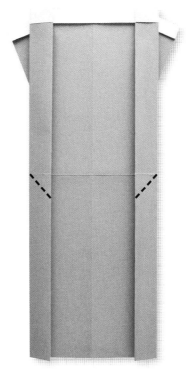

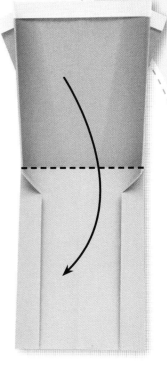

6 Make two new creases around ½ inch (13 mm) from either edge and fold the sides in.

7 Make two angled creases on these flaps. Press down firmly to flatten the paper.

8 Now valley fold the paper from top to bottom. Turn the paper over.

9

Use the folds you made in step 7 to shape the shoulders. Your suit jacket is now complete. Turn the page to learn how to make the bottom half!

PART 2

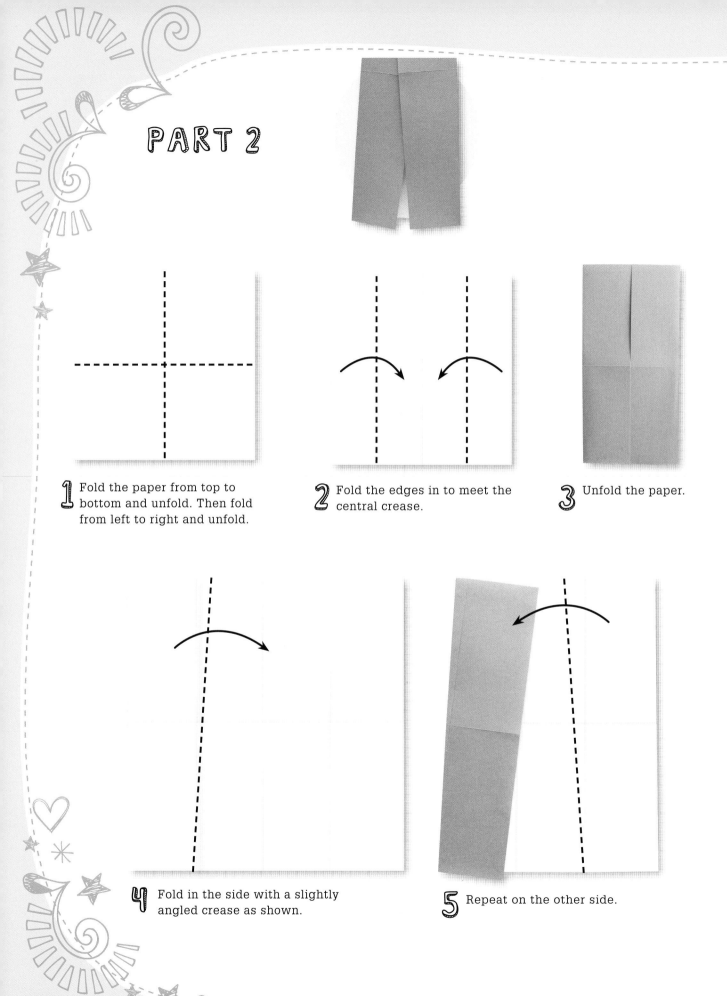

1 Fold the paper from top to bottom and unfold. Then fold from left to right and unfold.

2 Fold the edges in to meet the central crease.

3 Unfold the paper.

4 Fold in the side with a slightly angled crease as shown.

5 Repeat on the other side.

6 Mountain fold the edges at the same slight angle.

7 Mountain fold the top as shown.

8

Now the two parts of your suit are pressed and ready. Put them together and you have one stylish outfit all set for a night out!

Necktie

There are no tricky knots to master with this origami necktie. Follow the simple steps and you will have a fantastic result in minutes!

1

Place the paper as shown. Fold it in half from left to right and unfold.

2

Fold in the left and right edges from the top corner to meet the central crease.

3

Now you have a kite shape. Turn the paper over.

4

Valley fold the top so that the point lines up with the points on the left and right sides.

5

Fold up the tip as shown.

6

Make a crease just above the tip and fold the paper up once more.

28

7

Make two small angled creases on either side, as shown.

8

Turn the paper over.

9

Fold in the left and right edges to meet in the middle. Crease firmly over the layers at the top.

10

Turn the paper over.

11

Your necktie is now ready! Try drawing on a pattern of spots or stripes with a felt-tip pen to give your necktie some extra style.

Glossary

blouse A loose shirt often worn by girls and women.

bodice The top part of a dress, above the waist.

crease A line or mark made by folding something, such as a piece of paper. Also, to fold something so that a crease is formed.

garment An item of clothing.

gown A long dress, often worn for special or formal events.

horizontal Parallel to the horizon, at right angles to the vertical.

mountain fold A fold where the crease points up at you, like a mountain.

necktie A long piece of cloth that ties in the front and is worn around the neck.

valley fold A fold where the crease points away from you, like a valley.

vertical Straight up and down.

Further Information

Books

George, Lauren Delaney. *L. Delaney's All Dolled Up: Creating a Paper Fashion Wardrobe for Paper Dolls*. Mineola, NY: Dover Publications, 2017.

Song, Sok. *Everyday Origami: A Foldable Fashion Guide*. North Mankato, MN: Capstone Press, 2016.

Song, Sok. *Origami Outfits: A Foldable Fashion Guide*. North Mankato, MN: Capstone Press, 2016.

Websites

en.origami-club.com/clothes/index.html
This website uses diagrams and animations to show you how to make all kinds of origami clothes, from T-shirts to wedding dresses.

www.origami-make.org/howto-origami-kids.php
This website has instructions for making all sorts of origami creations, including shirts, pants, and a tote bag!

Publisher's note to educators and parents: Our editors have carefully reviewed these websites to ensure that they are suitable for students. Many websites change frequently, however, and we cannot guarantee that a site's future contents will continue to meet our high standards of quality and educational value. Be advised that students should be closely supervised whenever they access the Internet.

Index